Super Surfers

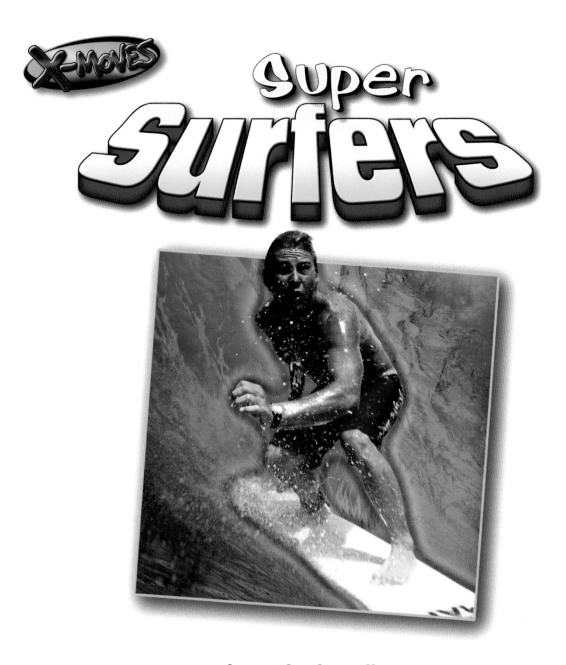

by Michael Sandler

Consultant: Jay DiMartino
Surfing Expert and Writer
www.surfing.about.com

BEARPORT
PUBLISHING

New York, New York

Credits

Cover and Title Page, © Pacific Stock/Superstock; TOC, © Sebastien Burel/Shutterstock; 5, © Robert Brown/ robertbrownphotography.com; 6, © North Wind Picture Archives/Alamy; 7, © The Bishop Museum Library & Archives; 8L, © Jonathan Blair/Corbis; 8R, © Bettmann/Corbis; 9, © The Bishop Museum Library & Archives; 10, © John Lyman Photos; 11T, © Joseba Etxaburu/Reuters/Landov; 11B, © Tim-McKenna/tim-mckenna.com; 12, © Copyright 2009/D Hump/aframephoto.com; 13, © Pierre Tostee/ZUMA Press; 14, © Quinn Rooney/Getty Images; 15, © Pierre Tostee/Reuters/Corbis; 16, © Jack English/ surfimages.com; 17, © Oscar Alonso Algote/envisionpublicidad; 18, © Tim-McKenna/tim-mckenna.com; 19T, © AP Images/Erik Aeder/Billabong; 19B, © Mike Segar/Reuters/Landov; 20, © Steve Robertson-ASP/Covered Images via Getty Images; 21, © Sergio Moraes/Reuters/Landov; 22T, © Tim-McKenna/tim-mckenna.com; 22B, © Lisa F. Young/Fotolia.

Publisher: Kenn Goin
Senior Editor: Lisa Wiseman
Creative Director: Spencer Brinker
Photo Researcher: Jennifer Bright

Library of Congress Cataloging in Publication Data

Sandler, Michael, 1965-.
  Super surfers / by Michael Sandler.
     p. cm. — (X-moves)
  Includes bibliographical references and index.
  ISBN-13: 978-1-59716-953-0 (library binding)
  ISBN-10: 1-59716-953-6 (library binding)
  1. Surfing—Juvenile literature. I. Title.

  GV840.S8S255 2010
  797.3'2—dc22

                                        2009007697

For more information, write to Bearport Publishing Company, Inc., 45 West 21st Street, Suite 3B, New York, New York 10010.

10 9 8 7 6 5 4 3

Contents

Into the Storm

During the first weekend of January 2008, a huge storm pounded the California coast. Wind knocked down trees. Rain flooded roads. Everyone stayed away from the ocean—except for **big wave surfers** like Mike Parsons, Brad Gerlach, Grant Baker, and Greg Long. They saw the chance of a lifetime in the storm. They hopped into a speedboat and raced across the sea.

Stopping at Cortes Bank, 100 miles (161 km) **offshore**, they jumped into the **massive** waves. For four hours, they surfed, **hurtling** down mountains of water at 45 miles per hour (72 kph). These were "the biggest waves of our lives," said Long.

CANADA

UNITED STATES

MEXICO

CALIFORNIA

Pacific Ocean

N
W   E
S

Cortes Bank

The Cortes Bank is a set of underwater mountains that rise up from the floor of the Pacific Ocean. In the right weather, the ocean water smacks into the mountains and creates towering monster waves.

In January 2008, Mike Parsons rode a wave greater than 70 feet (23 m) high, breaking the world record.

Surfing History

Surfing is one of the world's oldest extreme sports. It developed in Hawaii in around 1000 A.D. and quickly became a big part of everyday island life. When the waves rolled in, everybody surfed: kids, parents, even grandparents. Most people rode short boards. The long boards, called *olos*, along with the very best waves, were saved for kings and queens.

In 1778, explorer James Cook arrived in Hawaii. He became the first European to see surfing. In his journal, he wrote how shocked and amazed he was to watch people riding through water on wooden boards. It was from his writings that Europeans first learned about the sport.

Early surfers in Hawaii

Olo boards were so heavy that a team of servants had to carry them into the water.

This is one of the first known photographs of a surfer and his board. It was taken in 1890.

Surfing Around the World

In the early 20th century, the rest of the world began to discover surfing. First, Hawaiian wave riders such as Duke Kahanamoku brought the sport to California. Duke, an Olympic swimmer as well as a surfer, toured the world showing off his surfing skills.

Others found out about surfing during World War II (1939–1945). Many soldiers stationed in Hawaii returned home with surfboards. By the 1960s, surfing was turning into one of the world's coolest sports. Surfers became **celebrities**. They appeared on magazine covers and in movies. Competitions sprang up all over the globe.

Duke (in front) during a competition at Waikiki Beach in Hawaii

Surfers on a beach in 1965

Wooden surfboards were heavy, often weighing 100 pounds (45 kg) or more. In the 1950s, new lightweight **polyurethane** boards, weighing 40 pounds (18 kg) or less, were developed. They helped surfing grow more popular because they were easier to carry and better for doing tricks.

Duke was featured on a poster for the Mid-Pacific Carnival in 1914.

The Basics

Surfing is a pretty simple sport. A surfer paddles out into the water. Then he stops, floats while sitting on his board, and waits for a wave. When it comes, he begins paddling again—fast—in time with the wave's speed.

Finally, the wave catches the board. The surfer jumps up, as though he's doing a push-up, and then stands. Similar to a skateboarder or snowboarder, he rides using a side stance, with one foot forward and the other foot in back. His shoulder, not his chest, leads the way.

Now the surfer rides down or across the **face** of the wave. It's simple, but not easy. If he wipes out—falls off the board—then he will get **pummeled** by the water.

A group of surfers, such as this one, waiting to catch a wave is called the lineup.

Surfer Taj Burrow rides a wave.

Taj Burrow wipes out during a competition.

Australian Taj Burrow began surfing at age seven. Two years later, he won his first contest. Then, when he was 16 years old, he became Australia's junior champion. Today, Taj is considered one of the world's finest surfers. He's also one of Australia's best-paid athletes.

Surfing Moves

Surfers don't just ride waves. They also love to do tricks. In the 1960s, hanging ten toes over the **nose** of the board was a popular move. So was the cutback—turning the board around and riding back up toward a wave's breaking **curl**.

In the 1970s, tube riding became the sport's biggest thrill. A hollow tube of water is often created when a big wave curls. To tube ride, a surfer enters one end of this tube, rides through, and shoots out the other end.

In the last two decades, surfers have borrowed moves from snowboarders and skateboarders. Now, surfers are doing **tailslides**, **airs**, spins, and even flips, just like these other extreme athletes.

Champion surfer Silvana Lima shoots out of a tube.

Australian surfer
Joel Parkinson does
a backflip air.

To do an *air*, a surfer rides off a wave's
crest into the air and then lands back
down on the wave's face.

Competitions

Amateur surfing contests are found all around the world. Pro surfers test their moves in ASP World Tour events. These contests determine each year's surfing champions. They are held in such places as Hawaii, Brazil, California, Australia, and South Africa. These are the surf spots with the world's best waves.

In World Tour events, judges score surfers' rides on a scale of 1 to 10, with 10 being a perfect ride. What makes a ride a perfect 10? A surfer has to show speed, power, and smoothly link one move into the next.

Who rules the world tour? Layne Beachley and Kelly Slater! Layne has won seven women's titles, while Kelly has won nine men's titles.

Layne Beachley

Kelly Slater, shown here, is one of only two surfers to score two perfect 10s in a round in an ASP event. Joel Parkinson is the other.

Flying

While surfers can do airs in any competition, the best ones are seen at air shows. In these special contests, surfers aren't scored on how well they ride a wave's face. Instead, they are judged for the tricks they do in the air above the waves.

Surfers earn points for **grabs**, spins, and turning upside-down. Air specialists such as Bruce Irons, Josh Kerr, Jordy Smith, and Dayne Reynolds combine spins and flips into complex moves. These tricks have names such as the Kerrupt Flip, the Superman Air, and the 540 Rodeo.

Hawaiian surfer Bruce Irons performs a midair grab.

Bruce Irons during an air sequence

Bruce Irons is known for the height of his airs. He says, "I try to go as fast as I can and do the biggest air ever. I don't hold back."

Big Wave Riders

Many big wave surfers such as **legendary** rider Laird Hamilton skip contests altogether. Laird doesn't care for judging. "How do you judge art?" he asks. He also knows that monster waves aren't something you can schedule for a certain time or place.

The sea and weather have to be just right—as it was at Cortes Bank in January 2008—to create eight-story-high monsters. So the very best riders keep watch on the conditions for a chance to ride these special waves. Often, they are found at Northern California's Mavericks and at Hawaii's Jaws, the scariest **surf breaks** in the world.

Laird Hamilton catches a big wave.

For years, big wave surfers had a problem. Unlike small waves, the big ones move too fast for surfers to paddle into. In 1993, Laird solved this problem with the "tow-in." Surfers hang on to a towline attached to a Jet Ski. Speeding behind the Jet Ski, surfers can catch any size wave.

In 2004, Pete Cabrinha, shown here on the surfboard, took a world-record-breaking ride on a 70-foot (21-m) wave at Jaws. His record was broken in 2008 by Mike Parsons at Cortes Bank.

Pete Cabrinha

Braving Danger

Surfing can be risky. If surfers fall, they can hit rocks beneath the water and get hurt. Also, big waves can cause surfers to wipe out and drown. Laird remembers feeling "**vaporized**" by a monster wave at Jaws. Mark Foo, a top Hawaiian pro, drowned after wiping out on a wave at Mavericks.

Sharks are another threat surfers face. Perhaps because surfboards look like big fish, surfers attract their attention. Sharks seem to attack surfers more often than swimmers. For example, Bethany Hamilton, a top teen surfer from Hawaii, lost her arm in a shark attack.

Despite the risks, the thrill of riding will always keep surfers in the water. They'll keep trying to land the best new trick or catch the biggest wave.

Though Bethany Hamilton lost her arm in a shark attack, it hasn't stopped her from surfing.

Not all waves end in the ocean. Some surfers ride **tidal bore** waves like the pororoca in Brazil, where ocean tides sweep into rivers. These furious waves can create long-lasting rides of five miles (8 km) or more.

Brazilian surfer Noelio Sobrinho rides the pororoca tidal bore wave.

Surfing 101

Different surfboards are used for different styles of surfing. Short boards are better for making sharp turns and doing **aerial** tricks. Long boards are better for paddling into either very big waves or very small ones. Tow-in riders use surfboards with snowboard-style feet straps. No matter what kind of board they use, surfers know it's never safe to surf alone. That's why they always go into the water with a buddy.

Flotation Vest
Helps the surfer come back to the surface after a wipeout

Wet Suit
Keeps the surfer warm in cold water and protects the body against scratches and cuts

Tail
The back end

Deck
The top, where a surfer stands

Nose
The front end

Fins
Help the surfer guide a board

Rail
The edge of a surfboard

Leash
The cord that connects the surfer to the board

Glossary

aerial (AIR-ee-uhl) in the air

airs (AIRZ) tricks in which surfers ride into the air

amateur (AM-uh-chur) an event in which athletes don't receive money for competing; nonprofessional competitors

ASP (AY-ESS-PEE) the Association of Surfing Professionals; the group that runs pro surfing

big wave surfers (BIG WAYV SURF-urz) surfers who ride waves that are 15 to 20 feet (4.5 to 6 m) high

celebrities (suh-LEB-ruh-*teez*) very famous, well-known people

crest (KREST) the very top part of a wave

curl (KURL) the curved part of a breaking wave

face (FAYSS) the area of the wave on which the surfer rides

grabs (GRABZ) moves in which the surfer reaches down to grab the board while in the air

hurtling (HUR-tuhl-ing) moving at great speeds

legendary (LEJ-uhnd-*air*-ee) very famous

massive (MASS-iv) giant, huge

nose (NOHZ) the front tip of a surfboard

offshore (OFF-shor) out in the ocean, some distance from land

polyurethane (*pol*-ee-YOOR-uh-thayn) a foam material used to build surfboards

pro (PROH) a professional athlete; a person who is paid to play a sport

pummeled (PUHM-uhld) beaten, treated very roughly

surf breaks (SURF BRAYKS) sections of the ocean where waves form

tailslides (TAYL-slidez) tricks in which the surfer takes weight off the tail, or back end of the board, and slides it around quickly

tidal bore (TIDE-uhl BOR) a wave that is formed by an incoming ocean tide and travels up into a river, causing the water to run backward

vaporized (VAY-per-ized) made to vanish; completely destroyed

Bibliography

Casey, Susan. "Reef Madness." *Sports Illustrated* (January 21, 2008).

Marcus, Ben. *Surfing USA: An Illustrated History of the Coolest Sport of All Time.* St. Paul, MN: Voyageur Press (2005).

Warshaw, Matt. *The Encyclopedia of Surfing.* New York: Mariner Books (2005).

Warshaw, Matt. *Mavericks: The Story of Big-Wave Surfing.* San Francisco: Chronicle Books (2000).

Outside magazine

surfline.com

surfermag.com

Read More

Mason, Paul. *Ocean in Motion! Surfing and the Science of Waves.* Mankato, MN: Capstone (2009).

McClellan, Ray. *Surfing.* Minneapolis, MN: Bellwether (2008).

Sandler, Michael. *Bethany Hamilton: Follow Your Dreams!* New York: Bearport (2007).

Young, Jeff. *Kelly Slater.* Greensboro, NC: Morgan Reynolds (2008).

Learn More Online

To learn more about surfing, visit
www.bearportpublishing.com/X-Moves

Index